BORES

Published in Great Britain 1983 by
Private Eye Productions Limited
34 Greek Street, London W.1.

© Pressdram Limited

ISBN 233 97608 6

Also available:
Book of Bores
Star Bores

Filmset by
Metro Reprographics Ltd. London
Printed in Great Britain by
Butler & Tanner Ltd., Frome and London

PRIVATE EYE'S
BORES 3

Illustrations by Michael Heath

PRIVATE EYE

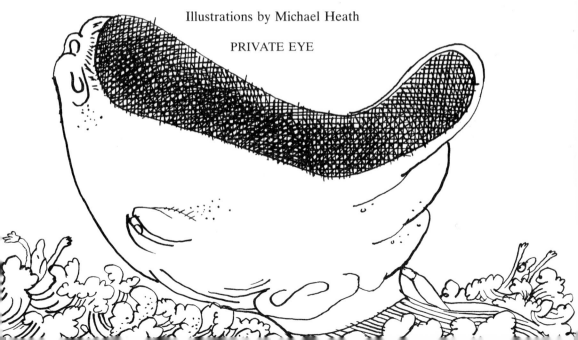

". . . I joined before the war it's frightfully convenient for me my office is only an hour or so's walk away and if you live in the country like I do it's very handy to have somewhere you can stay when you have to spend the night in town it only costs 25 guineas a night which is a lot cheaper than most hotels nowadays and if you want a nice quiet place to bring the wife after a show it's absolutely ideal now that they allow women in on alternate Tuesdays they've converted the old library into a ladies annexe yes there are quite a number of celebrities who come here there's that chap who plays the bank manager in that TV series and Robin Day I often see him in the bar he's much shorter than you imagine it costs me about £500 a year to belong which works out about a tenner a week bloody good value . . ."

". . . I bought this little number for Nigel at Christmas only £49 + VAT incredible value when you think of what treasures lie under the earth did you read that story the other day about the bank manager who went out to Epping Forest and found this Roman spear they think it is which is apparently priceless he had one of these identical to this mind you he can't keep it because by rights it belongs to the Crown hello! there she goes! when you get near a metal object it makes that whining noise you hear of course quite often it's milk bottle tops or something like that but Nigel found a ½ New Pee last week didn't you son?"

". . . no the only way to deal with these bastards is to bring hanging back like Enoch says they should it's the only thing buggers like that take any notice of a taste of their own medicine that's what they need and if they want somebody to do it I'd be more than 'appy to do the job myself I tell you if one of my nearest and dearest was killed by one of these animals and let's be perfectly frank that's what they are animals I'd line them up against the wall and chop them up into little bits the rope's too good for maniacs like that and that's what they are maniacs I think this Haritollah's got it right if someone rapes your little girl chop his whatsit off with a blunt axe make 'em think twice. . ."

". . . Capital Radio ONE-NINE-FOUR!!! hullo everybody I'm Sam the Sparkplug I'll put performance under your bonnet for half the price look out for me in the little yellow packet hullo there housewives I'm Winnie the Washing Machine just feed me full of hubby's soiled shirts and I'll wash 'em clean just watch me eat that dirt away because I'm biological pop down to your L.E.B. and pick me up! hullo everybody Monty here don't forget girls and boys I'm on your wavelength tonight and every night ring me with your problems and we'll all have a lovely chat ding! ding! ding! there's been a burst water main at Chiswick Flyover which is causing a massive tailback to the Hogarth Roundabout and an articulated lorry has overturned in Ladbroke Grove and the congestion round that area is very heavy indeed hullo everybody I'm Sam the Sparkplug. . ."

". . . I tell you she's a new woman since she started going to this clinic in Putney run by this American psychiatrist I can't remember his name anyway he thinks there's no such thing as mental illness and he's thrown all the preconceived theories out of the window she says there's a group of them and they all go along four times a week and shout the first thing that comes into their heads it's all based on the idea that when the foetus is in the womb it's unable to scream so everything gets bottled up in the subconscious apparently he encourages them to hit each other to get it out of their system Gavin goes along too and he's learning to accept her aggression and come to terms with it it's only fourteen guineas a session. . ."

". . . I could repair this for you sir but quite honestly I don't think it's worth my while quite frankly I'll do it if that's what you want but it's going to take time to get the parts for that particular model you see sir that is the '78 model and they've stopped making those now if you know someone who can supply the parts I can do the job but it's going to cost you and quite honestly you'd be better off buying a new one by the time you've got this one working again the decision is entirely yours sir this one is old sir you see and you're always going to have trouble with it whatever I do to it but it's up to you just say the word and I'll do my best I can't say fairer than that now can I. . . ?"

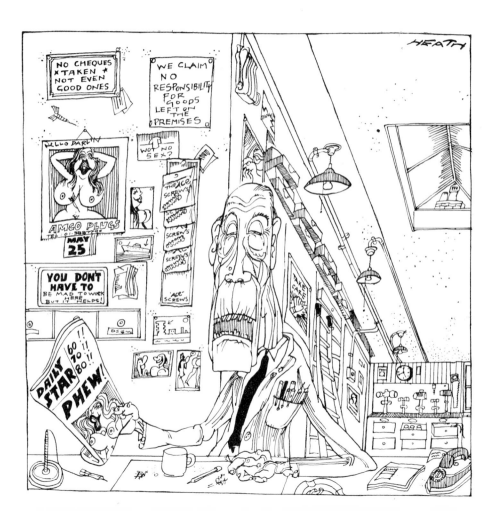

". . . no when you think what it was like when we first came here it's incredible you wouldn't believe it well you remember the Watsons used to grow mushrooms on it and it was just a mass of dandelions plantains and moss there was hardly a blade of grass to be seen I reckon those two tons of Fison's Superlawn have done the trick that and the nitrogen Growplus we put down in the winter it's like anything else a lawn give it care and consideration and it'll repay you a hundredfold I'm letting it breathe this summer and in the autumn I'm going to put on a layer of peat and Surrey loam and Percy Thrower's Vita-Grass and spray with ICI's Daisydeath you can't turn your back on it a lawn it's like anything else it's just as well we're not going away this year. . ."

". . . good afternoon ladies and gentlemen you are travelling on the 14:29 service from Charing Cross to Manchester calling at Didcot Oxford Banbury Leamington Wolverhampton Crewe Stoke-on-Trent and Manchester Piccadilly passengers for Guildford change at Tonbridge we regret that buffet facilities will not be available on this train due to staff shortages passengers leaving the train are requested to ensure that they take all items of baggage with them if passengers have any enquiries whatever about their journey please do not hesitate to ask me when I shall be passing through the train British Rail regret any inconvenience to passengers caused by the late departure of this train which was due to engineering works at Plymouth thank you ladies and gentlemen. . ."

"... after twenty-five years I think I have finally found the perfect way to make a really decent cup of coffee I've tried them all American percolators German filter papers Italian drip feed jobs French earthenware you know those brown things some people say you should just pour the water into a pot but I think you lose the flavour that way now this little beauty I found in a shop in Poland Street they import them direct from Mexico you put the ground coffee in the aluminium holder in the centre and pour the boiling water into this little spout in the corner and hey presto after about half an hour this whistle should go off hang on something's gone wrong here never mind I've got some Instant it's just as good I always say..."

". . . just look at that little beauty six cylinder four stroke water cooled engine and shaft drive electric start deep valence mudguards superlube oil injection I've had her pushing up to 135mph and not even a wobble on the forks you can't beat the double overhead camshaft plus I've had her fitted with quadruple carbs matt black pipes and chrome halogen lamps with stereo and rubberised suspension shafts you drive her out of the showroom around the two thousand mark juicy mind you she only does five to the gallon round town but I can push it up to ten on the motorway. . ."

". . . you know me I'm not religious in fact the last time I went to church was when your sister got married but I take my hat off to this new Pope Paul John John Paul whatever his name is from what I've seen of him on television he seems a first class bloke they talk about charisma don't they to tell the truth I don't know what it means but whatever it is he's got it in bucketfuls I mean a man of his age with all that energy picking kids up and waving them in the air I couldn't do half of what he does I think he's done a bloody good job and I say good luck to him mind you I don't agree with a lot of what he says but he's probably just doing what he's told he's got a job to do just like the rest of us. . ."

". . . did you see that programme the other night saying that drink damages the brain? what I say is this every time you cross the road you take your life in your hands if you get into a car you could be killed I reckon if you look at it that way you'd never get out of bed in the morning they say that even water can be poisonous my philosophy is that we're only here once and life is for the living I mean a little bit of what you fancy doesn't do you any harm why not enjoy yourself while you can and have a bit of fun? my old man drank a bottle of whisky every morning and smoked 60 Capstans a day and how old d'you think he was when he finally snuffed it? go on have a guess fifty-two? no even more than that eighty-three and what's more he died a happy man he was chuckling over a TV show at the time. . ."

". . . my dear I adore young people I won't hear a word said against them I think today's young generation are absolutely super so wonderfully uninhibited and interested in everything I only wish we'd had half their vitality when we were that age I mean today's young people are so refreshingly independent and so devastatingly frank about everything and such fun to be with and I adore the music so wonderfully loud and their clothes are so sensible and no one feels any silly guilt about things which is such a boon Rodney's just told his father he's living with another man and I'm so happy for him we told him darling it's your life make the best of it. . ."

". . . you must be mad doing your own return you should have my accountant I earned more money last year than I've earned in my life and he even got a rebate out of them I mean d'you realise you could be claiming for this flat not to mention the telly I manage to run two cars a new one every year not to mention the depreciation allowance plus petrol servicing etc my wife goes down as my secretary at £3000 per annum telephone bill is all accounted for he says he can even get a video system for nothing mind you he costs about £1000 a year but then that's deductible too what about haircuts do you claim for that? and that watch you've got to know the time haven't you?"

". . . I take my hat off to her quite frankly when you realise how old she is over 80 I think and still at it I mean I've got no time for most of them the way they carry on holidays in Mustique etc but I won't hear a word against her because I think she's a bloody marvel quite honestly she still goes racing and she's always got a smile d'you notice that? and she likes a drop or so I'm told and here's another thing she never wanted that job in the first place I mean when she married him she had no idea of what she was taking on but there you are I think if anyone apart from Churchill got us through the war it was her always smiling even during the Blitz she always had a smile for everyone. . ."

". . . have you ever worked out how much it costs to have your hair cut? I used to go once a fortnight to a little fellow just round the corner from the office nothing special short back and sides and a shampoo £6 no kidding that's what it costs me work that out for a year I'm talking about money real money so I said to the wife I said Beryl why don't you give it a go all you need is some clippers comb and that and would you notice the difference? no one does you should ask Audrey to do yours you could be sitting there just like me watching *Dallas* clip clip little drink in the hand £6 a fortnight work it out for a year it all adds up. . ."

". . . roads all completely deserted no one on the train couldn't get a paper anywhere if you ask me just because Monday was a bank holiday everyone's got it into their heads to take Tuesday off as well and I bet you anything you like some people will take the whole week off there seem to be more and more of these bank holidays every year Easter Monday May Day holiday and it will soon be Whitsun and the same thing will happen then another wasted week why don't they go the whole hog and give everyone a week off? it's the same at Christmas that more or less lasts for two weeks now if you count weekends apparently the average man only works five full weeks a year incredible no wonder the country's in a mess. . ."

". . . pretty cold isn't it? I'm afraid the Aqua-Thermo is on the blink and I'm sorry about all the green slime on the bottom I've had to put in this chemical stuff to disperse it and that's what makes the water taste so peculiar it's not very big I agree but then what with the water rates and the upkeep it costs a pretty penny I don't mind telling you and then there are so few days in our so-called British Summer when it's warm enough although I personally plunge in every morning before I get the train up to town and also when I get back in the evening we'll be away all July and August in the South of France I would love to have invited you to use it but I'm having it drained so that they can service the filter system and vacuum it you have to do it twice a year. . ."

". . . they're mad to leave him out quite honestly in my opinion after his century at Taunton last week 134 was it in just over 60 minutes I think it was I'd be the first to admit that he hasn't been on form as a bowler this season but then look at some of the others and the wickets they've been playing on have been giving no joy at all to the seamer I'd like to see him opening quite frankly he's wasted down the order look at that one-day against Northants did you see any of that? a fantastic game of cricket 279 was it they wanted? and three consecutive fours was it? and a five over long on. . ."

". . . isn't that a Blenheim? no it's an Avro Anson they made thousands of them before the war some of those African airlines are still running them amazing isn't it? still going strong after forty years they may be slow and uncomfortable to travel in but goodness me they're reliable I reckon it's the RC10 engines only 111 miles per hour top speed Smith Wharton air cooling system you don't often see them in this part of the world you can always tell the Avro Anson by the reinforced struts towards the rear of the fuselage hang on it's not an Avro Anson at all it's a Sopwith Talbot. . ."

". . . it's a little Maltese Terrier isn't it? they're lovely little dogs aren't they? my first husband had one of those called Champion when he lived in Dorking they're wonderful guard dogs aren't they? I bet you've never had burglars have you? not with this little chap to guard you mind you if I lived in the country I'd have a Bulgarian setter my aunt had one when she lived in Yorkshire but they need a lot of exercise and it isn't fair to keep them locked up in a service flat hasn't he got a little bit of Prince Charles Spaniel about him? I prefer a mongrel myself there's so much in-breeding nowadays isn't there? look what's happened to poodles my mother had a poodle. . ."

". . . 38 pounds worth of 5p pieces darling if you wouldn't mind two £5 bags of ½ ps could you put them into one of those plastic containers for me? thanks ever so much good Christmas? I bet you did how's that boyfriend of yours? that's right sweetheart £500 worth of 50ps can I have those in a bag? I haven't added up those cheques but I think you'll find they're all in order and could I have a new paying-in book on the second account and have you got a statement on the current account up to the 31st? only we seem to have got one cheque over any black ice down your way? can I borrow your biro for a second? I've just got to initial this Giro slip. . ."

". . .if you ask me the advantage of the microwave is basically the time aspect I mean we could go home now take something out of the deep freeze and it would be ready in no time at all Val's got one and she swears by it it's all very well for you Gerald but you don't appreciate the amount of time I have to spend in the kitchen I know it's a lot of money but you're bound to save in the end on electricity bills and to my mind all this health risk business is just eyewash I mean Val's had hers for two years and she's the healthiest woman I know and it's taken the drudgery out of her life I mean how many times have you said your lamb chop's lukewarm? all I'd have to do. . ."

". . . no I mean if someone wants to end it all surely they should have the right I think it's degrading for a human being to have to suffer unnecessarily in 1981 have you ever been into a geriatric ward? it's pathetic to see people reduced to that level of existence little better than vegetables I know that when my time comes I'll demand that the doctors provide me with the ways and means to end it all painlessly of course it's impossible to predict exactly what I would feel at the time but I'd like to have the option I knew this man who had a terminal illness. . ."

". . . and thanks to the silicon chip it is now possible for the Special Branch to tap every single phone in the country and store the information for future use er there is a computer centre we know at Hartley Wintney which contains statistics relating to every single vehicle so that for example it is possible for the police to know within seconds the identity of anyone who owns a car which represents the biggest threat to individual liberty ever known in 1966 for instance a Trade Unionist in Dunfermline who had once been a member of the Communist Party was stopped by a traffic patrol who accused him of being a terrorist that information could only have come from the Special Branch or Intelligence Service who are not publicly accountable now in America thanks to the Freedom of Information Act. . ."

". . . I'm alright on longsight I've got very good eyesight as far as things in the distance are concerned I can read a car number at 400 yards or so without any difficulty but I found I was having trouble reading the telephone directory and the wife said you should go and have a check up just to be on the safe side and the first thing the oculist asked me was how old are you and I said 42 and he said well that is the danger age when you get to 42 the retina muscles start to contract of course once you start wearing glasses it only makes things worse because apparently your eyes get slack and don't make the effort those are NHS frames aren't they I could have had those but I got these French designed bi-focals they cost a bomb but this man said where your eyes are concerned money shouldn't. . ."

". . . If you're going into hi-fi love its no use your thinking below two thou minimum that will just buy you the basics these days that means the simplest belt drive turn table but if you're thinking seriously about the whole outfit you're talking telephone numbers I mean I'm not thinking about anything but digital quadrophonic you can't buy this stylus anywhere I waited nine months for it to come from Japan and I slung out the four track tape-deck years ago this Akai is thirty two channels and the inbuilt impedance mike will pick up a blue bottle six streets away but the great thing is the speakers I've got eight of them and they're no bigger than cigarette boxes listen to this old Searchers album mind you it was made in mono but there's no surface sound at all. . ."

". . . you should have joined BUPA like me mate I've got my own room on the top floor with flexi visiting hours smashing nurses but the main thing is the total confidence in the one-to-one treatment you get with these blokes if I'd gone NHS with my complaint I'd still be on the waiting list in the year 2007 but as it was I only had to wait a week before they whisked me in here you see I'm a salesman and as the breadwinner my time is valuable now as a paid-up member of BUPA I can choose the time that suits ME they give you the full treatment body scan blood tests cardiogram all computerised mind you for an ordinary bloke that little lot would set you back a fortune but my firm pays for me so I mean it makes no difference. . ."

". . . ever done jury service? I had to go last week talk about a waste of time I thought all right a couple of days could do with a rest you must be joking couple of months it turned out to be you can't get out of it unless you can prove you're going abroad or some sort of disability first case comes up the bloke's obviously done it even the judge more or less says so we were all for having it over by dinner-time and I could get back to the office but this woman no way was she having it we tried for a majority verdict no way back again four nights in a hotel did you ever see that film *The Twelve Angry Men* with Henry Fonda? it was on the telly a few years ago bloody brilliant. . ."

". . . I used to think divorce would be terrible but quite the opposite is true when we were married we fought like cats and dogs now we're the best of friends it's unbelievable and the kids accepted it straight away they picked up the bad vibes kids are sensitive that way and they get on fantastically well with Penny that's my new wife and her children accept the new situation totally and her ex-husband is a good friend of mine as well as his new wife but the really exciting factor is that my ex hits it off really well with Penny in fact she's baby sitting for us this evening and the funny thing is I never fancied my ex when we were married but the other evening I went round there. . ."

". . . I never regretted for a moment the day we had the double glazing put in I know it costs a fortune but you're saving on your fuel bills and what with the price of fuel nowadays I reckon it's a real investment and when you come to sell your house it obviously puts the price up the other plus is the noise not that we get much living in the country you have to go into it very thoroughly before-hand of course there are plenty of ripoff merchants around in this game and it's not always the expensive ones who are the best we put this Danish system in ourselves and it doesn't spoil the look of the place you don't notice it after a day or two and it's a real deterrent in case of burglars no I never regretted it for a moment. . ."

". . . hullo! how's it all going tosh alright? good luck to you mate you're all right squire funny old world isn't it? wake up over there give us all a smile (*sings*) 'they tried to tell us we're too young too young to really be in love' what's the matter with you four-eyes? had a row with your wife? all right all right ALL RIGHT we know your sort think you know it all just cos you've got money you bleeding bastard you're all the same you! YOU! don't hide behind that newspaper give us a quid (*sings*) 'give me the last waltz with you'. . ."

". . . I don't know but I'll probably vote for the SDP next time I mean the other two parties have completely failed and I really think that these people do offer something different I have enormous respect and admiration for Shirley Williams who I think has shown tremendous courage and they're very good you know on housing and welfare and so forth it really is very exciting what they're doing making a real change in the whole political thing breaking up you know this old way they have of doing things and offering a genuine alternative you know that hasn't been tried before because everything the other parties have tried has just failed that's why I think we should all vote SDP. . ."

". . . just you taste this squire and I defy you to tell the difference between it and a 1968 Mouton Rothschild Premier Cru and d'you know what it cost me? this stuff works out at 2p a glass you can get all the equipment from Boots a standard kit costs around 25 quid which is all I use ie the plastic bin but you can just as well use an ordinary dustbin plus you get the powder of course any flavour you like I mean all you have to do is put the powder in the bucket siphon it through the little plastic whatsit leave it for three weeks but you can buy a Spanish one that only takes a couple of days with the price of drink nowadays it's money in the bank but for heaven's sake don't let a demi-john near a bottle of vinegar otherwise the whole lot is ruined by the way if you've got any spare bottles. . ."

". . . booking in at this place for Christmas is the best day's work I ever did because quite frankly another family affair would have driven me right round the bend just imagine your brother Reg and that wife of his and your mother getting all weepy as usual and besides it saves you all the cooking and all that wrapping up of presents not to mention the sheer cost of it all last year I reckon I spent two thou on gifts for the family alone and bloody kids running around and having to go next door and have a drink with that boring old so-and-so and none of that messy old Christmas tree cluttering up the lounge and pine needles all over the place I spent all last bloody Christmas trying to get the fairy lights going what's happened to room service where's that cocoa. . ."

". . . we find we both eat a lot more don't we Venetia? but we feel 100% fitter and we can actually taste the food which is fantastic you cannot ignore the figures in my view it's not just cancer it's all kinds of other illnesses as well apart from being anti-social I think it should be completely banned in public places like restaurants especially it's a statistical fact that if you spend three hours in the same room as people who are smoking it's the equivalent of having two high-tar cigarettes yourself they're complaining about too much tax but to my mind it's not nearly enough the price should be quadrupled so that it's completely prohibitive we've got a notice up on the door now and I just don't want to know people who want to kill themselves how would they like Venetia and me to go round to their place and breathe germs say if we had a contagious illness. . ."

". . . good way to go I just hope when it comes to my turn it'll be like that there he was in his armchair watching Little and Large his missus had just given him his Bournvita and then bang! good way to go he never knew what hit him best way isn't it really? I mean just imagine lingering on all those months in a hospital bed I'd hate to get into that state much better to get it over quickly Bang! you know just like that I mean he was working right up to the end he was in his allotment all day he'd gone dog racing in the evening sound as a bell walked back all of four mile and then bang! beautiful! good way to go. . ."

". . . alright so I was parked on the double yellow line I admit it but I was in the newspaper shop well how long does it take to buy a packet of papers and a couple of ounces of Old Holborn? anyway I came out of the shop and the car's gone I thought Christ it's been nicked not a bit it been towed away the other side of London Vauxhall car pound cost me a fiver to get there and they're asking forty quid plus the ticket which is another six quid needless to say I didn't have the cash so I ring the wife she's not there in the end it's half past two in the morning before we get away no wonder mugging's up 50% when you've got half a dozen coppers hanging around the car pound with nothing better to do than make other peoples' lives a misery. . ."

". . . fares please any more fares if you can afford 'em mum Brixton next stop get your passports ready only joking chocolate keep your 'air on what do you do put it in rollers? e's all right lady 'is brother's driving the bus got nothing smaller sir? American Express that'll do nicely cheer up guv it may never 'appen or in your case I think it already 'as what you got to look so cheerful about sonny won the pools or 'as the wife left you? any more fares please Clerkenwell madam? you want a 95 or a 38 'old very tight woops! don't blame me Lady Di isn't she luvelley mum I'd swop places with 'im any day 'ear about the Irishman. . ."

". . . Good god if it isn't Arbuthnot Minor I'd recognise the face anywhere you haven't changed a bit you were in Woodwards weren't you 28-33 I'm right aren't I? I'd recognise you anywhere you used to share a study with Pickering didn't you? d'you know I met him the other day just the same he's something in glass fibre East Grinstead way done very well for himself he scored 103 against the Old Boys don't you remember? did you see that old Donaldson had died? surely you remember him? he could touch the end of his nose with his tongue don't you ever go back? I was there only last month guess who the first person I saw was? Reggie Thickett his boy's there now in your old house would you believe it? surely you remember him? he was in the Remove when you got caught smoking by old Fieldgate really? oh I'm awfully sorry funny I could have sworn well you look just like him. . ."

". . . have you ever had that funny feeling you've been somewhere before? I mean there's so many things we don't really understand I think a lot of houses have an atmosphere of their own you sense it as soon as you go in I've never seen a ghost myself but I don't necessarily disbelieve in them a friend of mine was staying in this old hotel up in the Midlands this was way back during the war he'd just gone to bed when he saw this dog walk right through the door and the next day he got talking to the landlord and he said I didn't know you had a dog and the landlord said oh you saw the dog did you? did you know there was an old man who stayed in that room apparently about 50 years before and he had this dog devoted to it he was and one day. . ."

". . . no question about it he is the master of suspense did you see that one last night? apparently that scene in the shower where the girl gets stabbed if you look at it carefully you'll see that the knife never actually touches the body amazing isn't it? do you remember in that other film when the bloke is stuck out in the middle of Arizona and he's chased by this aeroplane and there's nowhere for him to hide did you know he appeared in every single one of his films that was his trademark I couldn't see him in the one last night my wife said he was the Frenchman on the bicycle with the string of onions what was the name of that film when they try to murder a man in the middle of a concert at the Albert Hall that was fantastic. . ."

".. . phew! wow! waddya know? I just can't believe it words fail me no seriously what can I say? just that I never for a moment expected to get this magnificent token of your esteem I'd just like to say a big thank you to my co-star who really is the one who should be up here tonight but also to the producer Cyrus J. Hooberman who can't be with us unfortunately he's in hospital in Los Angeles and I hope he's watching this on satellite Hi! Melve! get well soon! but seriously I would like to thank also the production crew all the people who worked so hard behind the scenes and my agent Barry Cosmo who has never lost faith in me and of course my wife Rowenta well words fail me just thank you God bless you darlings you really are the sweetest people God bless you all I love you and I really mean that.. ."

"... £185,000 a year it may sound a lot of money to you but by the time the Taxman gets his sticky little fingers on it it's literally more than halved then you've got to take into account what it costs in terms of accountant's fees tax advisers then there's the life insurance that costs a fortune school fees and my first wife I'm still paying the mortgage off on that place that's 300 grand and how much do you think it costs to run a Lamborghini? the servicing alone is worth a mini Metro it's crippling I'll be lucky if by the end of the year I break even take a chap like you probably on £150 a week you're a lot better off I'd swop places with you any day leaving already? my driver will take you home..."

". . . and I said to him I'll meet you in the Zanzibar at half past eight and he rings me up at six o'clock because he's got to meet this Paul person somewhere in the City anyway he rings up again obviously he wasn't at the office because I could hear the laughing so I said to him are you coming or aren't you because I'm not going to stay here all night waiting for you so then he said he'd pick me up at half past eight at Foxtrot Oscar so I get a cab and still no sign would you believe it was half past two in the morning after I'd got back the phone rings and it's guess who? I said to him where have you been and what time do you think this is? well he only wants to bring this Paul round so I said to him. . ."

". . . I wouldn't be without it now it's fantastic the difference it makes one feels so much better I started originally with the underwear but I have everything thermal now gloves socks everything apparently it's made out of this stuff called Thermolactyl which allows sweat to pass through and it builds up this electric heat you notice it when you take your vest off in the dark you can see the sparks of course they've been using it for years for mountaineering polar expeditions and all that sort of thing you can get it all in Marks and Sparks both the boys have got it and Gerald too it's amazing and the saving on the heating is just incredible. . ."